BURMA

BURMA

Encountering the Land of the Buddhas

Ellis Everarda

Paul Strachan

KISCADALE

Nothing of what I imagined had prepared me for the worship and devotion of the Burmese people for the Lord Buddha. In this golden country everything is joined together in reverence of Him.

PREFACE

Burma, like a slow burning love affair, draws its beholder into a world of beauty and strangeness. Here is a culture formed by the union of the teachings of Lord Buddha and the devout people of that land, with ways of thinking and refined manners unique to them.

During many visits to Burma I was moved by a creative force in search for a new kind of beauty. Gradually I opened to the vitality and warmth of the people in this insulated country. At the same time it was difficult to close my eyes to social and political questions. Perhaps, deliberately I chose not to focus on these in my work. For, on the positive side, Burma has preserved something which most countries have lost and whilst the Burmese people are aware of the reality of the country's state of affairs, they have learnt to soothe their minds in something that lies beyond the world of concepts and words. They speak about that which is truer to life, conceptions that less flexible Western minds cannot so easily grasp.

At moments pen and camera shared experiences, at others times they lived lives of their own. Both tried to arouse that sense of distant beauty. These impressions are subjective, distilled from the people's daily way of living with the Buddha's teachings. As the country moves towards a new future I have done my best to present a portrait of a timeless Burma.

This book is for Ko Maung Maung who lives near the Ananda temple in Pagan. With his spontaneous spirit he guided me through his beloved country, instilling in me a love of things Burmese. Without trying to be complete, I began to unravel the large tapestry that is Burma. I hope that for those who have already, and for those who have yet to succumb to the tempting voice of Burma, this book is a memory of scenes, smells and sounds.

Ellis Everarda
Hong Kong, 1994

Rangoon, the Capital• 11

Con

Mandalay, the Royal City • 35

Published in 1994 by Paul Strachan - Kiscadale publications ltd, Ancaster Business Centre, Cross street, Callander, Fk17 8dx, Scotland

Land and Water • 59

ents

Pagan, The Sacred Plain • 85

Rangoon, the capital

The Shwedagon

When visiting the Shwedagon footwear, out of respect, must be left down below and it is necessary to walk barefoot up the dirty floors of the long covered stairs. It is best to walk slowly, in tune with the gentle throng of worshippers who come to offer alms and flowers to the Buddha. On reaching the summit the warm sun strikes and suddenly a world of crystalline temples unfolds. To the centre the great golden pagoda rises into the sky. The air is filled with the tinkle and jingle of thousands of little bells. Sitting alone in a quiet corner shaded by a banyan tree one can watch the people floating by. The atmosphere is exotic yet serene.

The immense stupa is surrounded by innumerable smaller golden and silver pagodas. There are pastel coloured shrines and glass mosaic prayer halls. Some of the temples are decorated with ecstatically carved wood, others with glowing lacquer. Countless images of the Buddha, lesser deities and demons are sitting in grand conclave about the platform. A woman strikes the bell. Some people pray for hours, stilling their minds. Others offer candle-sticks, paper umbrellas and flowers or regild the pagoda with thin sheets of gold leaves. Smiles soften lips. Everybody seems to carry out meaningful actions within well established temple rules.

With a prayer flag this frail nun sends her message to heaven. The religious words she knows by heart. As a child she has gone over them again and again. Now they flow from the mind to the lips without pausing. Having first made her circumambulation of the main shrine this spot was chosen to pray at. It is the shrine dedicated to the day of the week on which she was born, of great astrological importance.

For the devout layman the sanctity of the pagoda begins at the first of the hundred and eighty pagoda steps. The sweet fragrance of incense sticks and flowers will waft him up. Re-arranging his 'longyi' when he arrives at the platform he first strikes the big bell and summons the attention of the deities to his prayers. Then he takes out his prayer beads and walks bare-foot around the platform on the night-cooled marble. By the time the sun is high above the horizon he is drawn to a peaceful pavilion to recite the scriptures. It is held that accumulated merit can be transmitted to another cycle of existence. And thus before going down the same steps, he places incense in a brass pot and affixes gold leaves to the pagoda, giving it a heavenly glow.

16

Downtown...

Rangoon, baking in the sun, moves with a gentleness that does not belong to a capital city. To the patter of velvet slippers, the immaculately dressed crowds stroll. Ever mindful of traditional ways and appearances, the people make up for the facades that cry out for paint and restoration. The fine tenements, erected by the British Raj, are now overflowing offices.

23

M andalay, the Royal City

The ancient Mandalay train leaves Rangoon at six in the morning and takes an almost straight line through the central plains of Lower and Upper Burma. For twelve hours an arid heat accompanies and as the afternoon wears on it steadily grows heavier. Each compartment is filled with a torpor. Peoples' faces become muddied with dust and sweat. Outside endless rice fields merge with a flat horizon. It is time to reap the harvest and the ripe golden stalks simmer beneath the sun. Once in a while the horizon is broken by the distant low hills that circle the plains and the occasional white-washed stupa can be seen perched on a summit.

Mandalay Hill...

From the Mandalay Hill the plain stretches from the blue Shan hills in the East to the banks of the Irrawaddy river in the West. At the top of the hill stands a magnificent statue of Buddha's disciple Ananda. He points his finger towards the site where King Mindon's fabled palace once stood. The legend goes that Ananda prophesised that on the 2,400th year after the Lord Buddha's birth there would be a city founded on this spot and it would become the Centre of the Universe. The vestiges of Mandalay's glorious past have vanished, razed by fire and war, yet the magic remains.

The Kuthodaw...

The Kuthodaw pagoda is a silent place. Within the walls echoes of bare footsteps can be heard above the soft jingling of metal 'bo' leaves. The silence is planned as is everything in the compound from the design of the temple to each stone slab sheltered within its own separate pavilion. Even the broad trees that offer shade were part of the founder's plan. Each of the epigraphs bear a 'page' of the world's largest book, the Buddhist 'Tipitaka'. It once took 2,400 monks one hundred and fifty days to read all 1,460 pages. If one man spent eight hours a day to read the scriptures he would be occupied for four hundred and fifty days. Good shade is thus necessary.

41

Ava…

Near to the former capital of Ava villagers assemble to dedicate a new pagoda. Theirs is not an ostentatious love for riches. Rather their finery is an expression of a spiritual bond, a religious gesture of the devout: for in Burma material wealth is always subordinated to spiritual wealth. As his life draws to a close, any man who has achieved good fortune builds a pagoda. In doing so merit is acquired for himself, his family and all humanity, paving the way for all to Nirvana. At such celebrations all, whether in royal robes or daily 'longyi', come to the pagoda to offer new Buddha images and flowers or to light candles - each an act of merit .

46

Sagaing...

The road from Mandalay to Sagaing is like the overture of an opera, the real performance has yet to come. The route is studded with are shrines, pagodas and other religious structures. Early sounds of chanting come and go from the monasteries. In robes of saffron and scarlet novices make their alms rounds, kindling the hearts of the devout. From the craftsmens' quarter images of the Buddha in wood, marble and bronze bless the pilgrims on their peregrination towards Sagaing. The one and only bridge over the mighty Irrawaddy river at the former capital Ava spans the incandescent waters and the Arcadian Sagaing hills are capped with the finials and spires of inestimable numbers of shrines and monasteries. If Mandalay is the cultural heart, then Sagaing is the spiritual heart of Burma.

Land and Water

The women sell in the markets and tend their cooking
pots whilst the men go out fishing. Fish, whether from
the magnificent Irrawaddy or from the shimmering Inle
Lake, is a major source of food and a valuable source
of income to many. Nets, either suspended from booms
or cast from craft are for a few moments lowered into
the waters and raised sparkling silver with catch. Fish
are abundant and men and women side by side make
and mend the nets in the evening, just before the sun
prepares to go down.

The Irrawaddy...

From high in the Himalayas to the depths of the south-
ern delta the Irrawaddy, great artery of Burma, pumps
life into the nation. Fish, irrigation and navigation
have for centuries commanded the economy. Many people are born into long lines of navigators, their vessels
their homes, plying vast distances to transport wares
such as these water pots from one end of the land to the
other. In the monsoon the waters rise several meters
high and the river swells to miles wide. In the heat of
April and May it dwindles to a meandering trickle
through deserts of sand dunes.

Inle…

Truly this must be the Venice of the East. On Inle Lake people can row before they can walk. Here men live more in harmony with water than land. Even the plantations and market gardens are floating - barges of bamboo and earth bobbing on the surface. Each market day villagers paddle into the central village of He-ye-ywa-ma to exchange wares. Even the pagoda processions and festivals are conducted upon the incandescent waters.

Kalaw...

The Padaungs...

The Padaungs are Burma's brass-necked women. Their heads sway high above layers of gleaming coils as if only tenuosly attatched to their sloping shoulders. Their bodies look unnaturally petite above long brass-covered legs as they go barefoot in their home-spun rags. A piece of cloth is wrapped around their hair and another piece is tied beneath the collar to protect the roasting skin from sores and diseases.

From the age of five Padaung women go through their first neck ringing ceremony and over the years further brass rings are added stretching the neck longer. A single woman can carry over 45kg of metal, a third of it about the neck. the remaining pounds around her legs. This ringing may have begun as a protection against tigers who once infested the jungle. If a woman is caught breaking her marriage vows then the coils are removed and her head will wobble from side till, unsupported, she will die.

Pagan, the Sacred Plain

Today more than two thousand monuments have been counted but according to one inventory made in the 18th century there was once more than double this. Since then earthquakes and climate have taken their toll. Built between the 11th and 14th centuries AD the site covers an area of nearly sixteen square miles of arid, deserted plain. Each monument was an act of merit, the great temples of kings, the lesser ones of ordinary people. To this day all serve to glorify the faith as they were intended to by their founders. There are a terrific variety of forms and styles though nearly all are built of brick. Many house fine paintings and sculptures of stone and stucco. Pagan has never failed to uplift Buddhist and non-Buddhist alike.

Though Pagan, said to have been sacked in 1287 by the Mongols, has long ceased to be Burma's capital it is no dead city. In the 18th and 19th centuries successive kings from Ava and Mandalay recognised their historical and cultural debt to this the seat of Burma's first empire. Many spent lavishly on new monasteries or renovated existing temples, often adding schemes of mural paintings, quite different in style to the original works. To this day there remains an active cultural life in the villages of the Pagan plain with processions and festivals for any occasion. Opera troupes and carnivals are for ever arriving for various of the many pagoda festivals. The villagers themselves are famed for their manufacture of high quality lacquer and dexterity at puppeteering.

ILLUSTRATIONS

Frontispiece	Buddha, Sulamani Temple, Pagan	33	Novice at Rangoon Kyauk-taw-gyi reclining
Preface	Bullock cart, Pagan		Buddha
10	Buddhist nun at the Shwedagon	34	The paddy harvest
11	Water melon seller, Rangoon	35	Sweet seller on the Mandalay Express
12	Stupas in the enclosure of the Shwedagon	36	Old lady puffs on cheroot
13	Platform and terraces, Shwedagon	37	Mandalay taxi and horse cart
14	Detail of bronze seated Buddha, Shwedagon	38/39	Standing Buddha, Mandalay Hill
15	Pilgrim strikes bell to inform the nats of her act	40/41	Novice reads at Kuthodaw pagoda, Mandalay
	of merit, Shwedagon	42	Stage coach taxi, Maymyo
	Ceremonial offering to the nats, Shwedagon	43	Kyauk-taw-gyi pagoda, Mandalay
16	Buddhist nun with prayer flag, Shwedagon	44	Crowned Buddha
17	Lay devotee offers gold leaf to the Shwedagon	45	Procession of monks on their alms round
18	Novices and bonfire	46/47	Offering of a new Buddha, Ava
19	Interior of main shrine, Shwedagon	48	Traditional puppets
20	Meeting of trustees and monks	49	The road to Sagaing
21	Lesser stupas around the Shwedagon	50	Umin Thonze pagoda, Sagaing
22	Monks make ritual circumambulation	51	The Ava bridge
23	Downtown tenement	52	Novices after collecting alms
24	Female pilgrim, Rangoon	53	Nuns
25	Old Rangoon house, Boundary Road	54	Kaung-hmu-daw pagoda, Sagaing
26	Noodle stall, Rangoon	55	The bells on a pagoda finial or *hti*
27	Feeding pigeons	56	Elder in charge of a pagoda donation office
27	Melon sellers	57	Novice
28	Rangoon belles	58	Fishing boats on the Irrawaddy
29	Fortune teller	59	The fish seller
30	Bridal couple	60	Mending the nets
31	Bridesmaid and page	61	In the river!
32	Monks after the alms round	62	Evening ablutions

63/64	Nets
65	U Bein Bridge, Amarapura
66/67	Water pots
68	Old lady carries lacquer offering receptacle
69-71	On Inle lake
72-74	The Inle market
75	An 'Inthu' or lady of Inle
76	'Intha' or man of Inle
77	Fishing boats with traps on Inle
78	Boy and bullock cart
79	Pa-o woman at the Kalaw market
80	Horse cart, Kalaw
81	Pa-o breastfeeding her baby
83	Padaung women
84	Bullock cart traffic, Minnanthu
85	Naga-yon temple
86	Farm life, Pagan village
87	That-byin-nyu temple
88	Ananda temple
89	North Buddha, Ananda
90	Relief sculpture in Ananda portraying the escape of the bodhisattva from his palace
91	Twilight over the Nagayon and Abeyadana temples
92	The Pagan plain from the Min-gala-zedi pagoda
93	Standing Buddhas, Pagan
94	Small temple, Pagan
95	The twin Buddhas, Dhama-yan-gyi south shrine
96	19th century wall painting, Sulamani temple
97	Arrival at the Sulamani
98/99	Classical dancing, pagoda festival at Pagan
100	Offerings to pagoda guardian, Shwe-zigon
101	Clown performs at the Shwe-zigon
102	Collecting water, Pagan Wetkyi-in
103	Young monks
104	Empty throne, Nanda-min-nya temple
105	Carts on the Ananda road
106	Old lady smoking, Pagan village
107	The Bu-hpaya
108	A young girl with a pagoda offering
109	Contemporary painting by Shwe Kyaw Lin of a pagoda festival procession
110	Pagan girl
111	Crowned Buddha
112	The Shwedagon after dusk